Country ABCs

France ABCs

by Sharon Katz Cooper   illustrated by Stacey Previn

A Book About the People and Places of France

Special thanks to our advisers for their expertise:
Christophe Veltsos, Ph.D.
Minnesota State University, Mankato

Susan Kesselring, M.A., Literacy Educator
Rosemount–Apple Valley–Eagan (Minnesota) School District

PICTURE WINDOW BOOKS
Minneapolis, Minnesota

Editor: Jill Kalz
Designer: Nathan Gassman
Page Production: Angela Kilmer
Creative Director: Keith Griffin
Editorial Director: Carol Jones
The illustrations in this book were created in watercolors.

Picture Window Books
5115 Excelsior Boulevard
Suite 232
Minneapolis, MN 55416
877-845-8392
www.picturewindowbooks.com

Printed in the United States of America.

Library of Congress Cataloging-in-Publication Data
Cooper, Sharon Katz.
France ABCs : a book about the people and places
of France / by Sharon Katz Cooper ; illustrated by
Stacey Previn.
p. cm. — (Country ABCs)
Includes bibliographical references and index.
ISBN 1-4048-1568-6 (hardcover)
1. France—Juvenile literature. 2. Alphabet books.
[1. France. 2. Alphabet.] I. Previn, Stacey, ill. II. Title.
III. Series.
DC33.C638 2005
94—dc22   2005021811

Bonjour! (bohn-JOOR)

That's how people say "Hello!" in French. France is a country in Europe. More than 60 million people live there. France is known around the world for its food, fashion, art, and wine.

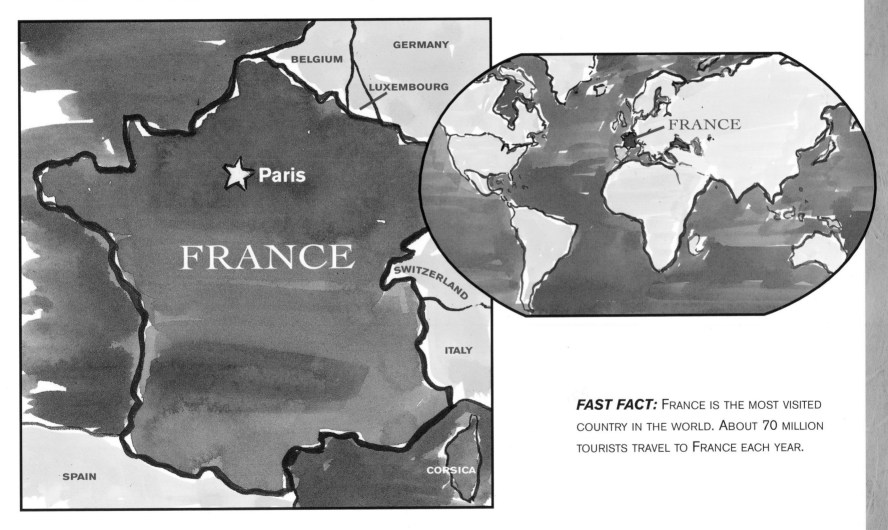

FAST FACT: FRANCE IS THE MOST VISITED COUNTRY IN THE WORLD. ABOUT 70 MILLION TOURISTS TRAVEL TO FRANCE EACH YEAR.

A is for art.

France is famous for its art and artists. Some of the oldest paintings in the world are in the caves of Lascaux. Prehistoric people painted animals on the cave walls. Thousands of years later, masterful painters such as Pierre Auguste Renoir, Claude Monet, Edgar Degas, and Paul Cézanne called France their home.

B is for Bastille Day.

Held on July 14, Bastille Day is one of the most important holidays on the French calendar. It marks the anniversary of the French Revolution (1789–1799), which brought an end to the French monarchy. Today, people celebrate Bastille Day with parades, picnics, bonfires, and fireworks.

C is for cheese.

French people eat more cheese than any other people in the world. Each person eats about 45 pounds (20 kilograms) of cheese per year! More than 400 different kinds of cheese are made in France. Cheese can be made from cow's milk, goat's milk, or sheep's milk.

FAST FACT: A FRENCH NEIGHBORHOOD CHEESE SHOP IS CALLED A *FROMAGERIE* (FROH-MAHJ-UH-REE), FROM THE FRENCH WORD FOR CHEESE, *FROMAGE* (FROH-MAHJ). EACH SHOP MIGHT SELL MORE THAN 200 KINDS OF CHEESE.

Dd

Charles de Gaulle was a French general during World War II (1939–1945). While Germany controlled France, de Gaulle urged the French to fight for their freedom. Finally, on June 6, 1944 (D-Day), de Gaulle and his troops joined the Allied forces to free the country. After the war, de Gaulle became the prime minister and then president of France.

FAST FACT: THE LARGEST AIRPORT IN PARIS IS THE PARIS ROISSY CHARLES DE GAULLE AIRPORT. MORE THAN 200,000 PASSENGERS PASS THROUGH IT EACH DAY.

D is for de Gaulle.

E is for Eiffel Tower.

The Eiffel Tower, in Paris, is one of the most famous monuments in the world. Designed by a French engineer named Gustave Eiffel, the Eiffel Tower opened for visitors during the 1889 World's Fair. With more than 1,600 steps, the Eiffel Tower stands 1,056 feet (320 meters) high—taller than most 80-story buildings!

FAST FACT: MORE THAN 200 MILLION PEOPLE HAVE VISITED THE EIFFEL TOWER.

F is for flag.

The French flag is blue, white, and red. Blue stands for fraternity, white stands for equality, and red stands for liberty. During the French Revolution, people fought for freedom and equal rights for everyone. The French have flown this flag since 1794.

G is for Guerande.

The salt marshes of Guerande are in the region of Brittany, on France's west coast. Farmers today still harvest sea salt from the low, wet land the traditional way—by hand. Because of the large number of egrets, purple herons, and other birds that live there, the salt marshes are a nationally protected area.

H is for Hugo.

Victor Hugo was a famous 19th-century French author. He wrote poetry, stories, and essays. His most famous novels are *The Hunchback of Notre Dame* and *Les Miserables*.

I is for impressionism.

Impressionism is a style of painting. It became popular in France in the late 1800s. Impressionist painters used dabs of color to show their subjects. They tried to create moods rather than life-like images. Degas, Monet, and Renoir are famous impressionist painters.

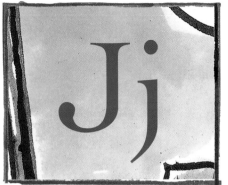

Jj

J is for Joan of Arc.

Joan of Arc was a French military leader in the 1400s. She was only 17 years old when she helped to chase English troops from a captured French town called Orleans. She made many battle plans for the French military.

FAST FACT: FRENCH PEOPLE THOUGHT JOAN WAS AN ANGEL, BUT PEOPLE IN ENGLAND THOUGHT SHE WAS A WITCH. WHEN THE ENGLISH FINALLY CAUGHT HER, THEY BURNED HER AT THE STAKE.

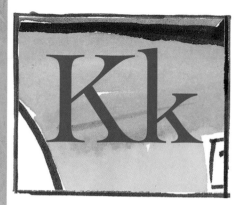

K is for kilogram.

France, like many other countries around the world, uses the metric system of measurement. The French weigh things using kilograms.

FAST FACT:

A KILOGRAM IS EQUAL TO 2.2 POUNDS.

L is for lavender.

Summer visitors to the Provence region in France will see many purple fields. These fields are filled with lavender, a plant with small purple flowers. Lavender blooms from late June to mid-October. Many people think it has a very relaxing smell. Lavender is often used in soaps and perfumes.

M is for museum.

France has nearly 1,200 museums. One of the most important is the Louvre (below), in Paris. It holds more than 1 million paintings, sculptures, and other objects. Another famous art museum in Paris is the Musee d'Orsay. It was built in an old railway station.

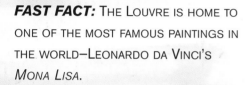

FAST FACT: THE LOUVRE IS HOME TO ONE OF THE MOST FAMOUS PAINTINGS IN THE WORLD—LEONARDO DA VINCI'S *MONA LISA*.

N is for Napoléon.

Napoléon was sent to military school at the age of 9. He became one of France's greatest leaders after the French Revolution.

FAST FACT: Napoléon had workers start building the Arc de Triomphe in Paris in 1806. The massive stone arch was meant to celebrate Napoléon's leadership and his armies' bravery.

O is for ocean.

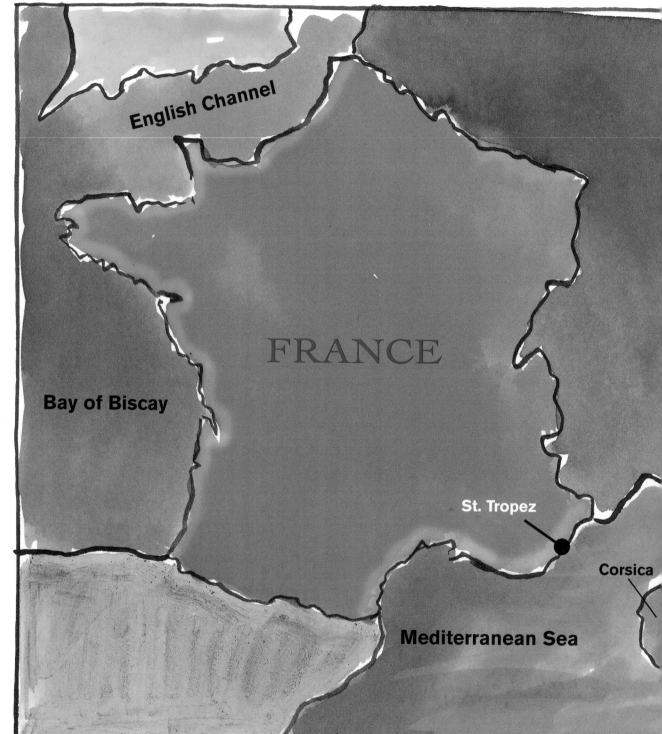

English Channel

Bay of Biscay

FRANCE

St. Tropez

Corsica

Mediterranean Sea

Three large bodies of water border France. The English Channel borders France's northwest coast. The Bay of Biscay lies to the west. The Mediterranean Sea lies to the south and surrounds the island of Corsica. All three bodies of water are parts of the Atlantic Ocean.

FAST FACT: FRANCE HAS MANY BEAUTIFUL BEACHES. THE MOST POPULAR BEACHES, SUCH AS ST. TROPEZ, ARE ALONG ITS MEDITERRANEAN COAST.

P is for Paris.

Paris is the capital of France. It is known for its cafés, fancy restaurants, museums, and architecture. The Eiffel Tower, the Louvre, and Notre Dame Cathedral are in Paris. The Seine River runs through the city, dividing it into the Right Bank and the Left Bank.

FAST FACT: PARIS IS OFTEN CALLED THE CITY OF LIGHTS.

19

Q is for quoi (KWAH).

Quoi means "what" in French. More than 113 million people speak French fluently worldwide. French is spoken as a native language on five continents. Many French words have become a part of English, including blond, cuisine, matinee, and petite.

cuisine

matinee

blond

petite

FAST FACT: FRENCH IS THE 11TH MOST COMMON FIRST LANGUAGE IN THE WORLD.

R is for Riviera.

The French Riviera is a coastal region of France. It borders the Mediterranean Sea. It has sunny beaches, mountains, museums, and unique food. The French Riviera is a favorite vacation spot, both for the French and for people from many other countries.

S is for style.

France is the world's center for fashion and style. Many clothing designers work in France. Every January and July, models show off the newest fashions in two big shows in Paris. Very trendy and imaginative clothes are called haute couture (OAT koo-TOOR).

T is for Tour de France.

The Tour de France is a famous bicycle race that winds through France. It follows a different route every year, but it always ends in Paris. The 3,700-mile (5,920-kilometer) race is biked in 21 to 24 stages, and it lasts through the month of July. The lead cyclist is always given a yellow jersey to wear.

FAST FACT: LANCE ARMSTRONG, AN AMERICAN CYCLIST, WON THE TOUR DE FRANCE EVERY YEAR BETWEEN 1999 AND 2005.

23

U is for Union.

Uu

France is a part of the European Union (EU). The EU is a group of 25 European countries that work closely together and share resources. Many EU countries use the same unit of money, called the euro.

V is for Versailles.

Versailles was the home of King Louis the 14th, who reigned from 1643 to 1715. It was built to be the largest and grandest palace in Europe. The king used the 700-room palace to entertain other kings and royalty. Today, the palace is open for tours and cared for as a national treasure.

FAST FACT: THERE ARE 200,000 TREES AND 50 FOUNTAINS ON THE GROUNDS OF VERSAILLES. GARDENERS PLANT MORE THAN 200,000 FLOWERS EACH YEAR.

W is for wine.

Wine is a beverage made from the juice of grapes. Many people consider France to be the best wine-making country in the world. There are vineyards throughout the country. Every region has its own special wines.

FAST FACT: BURGUNDY, BORDEAUX, AND CHAMPAGNE ARE ALL FAMOUS WINE-MAKING REGIONS IN FRANCE.

X is for ibex.

The Alpine ibex is a rare wild goat that lives high in the French Alps. Much of its habitat was lost years ago when people built ski resorts in the mountains. The French government has recently created national parks to protect the animals and give them a safe place to live.

27

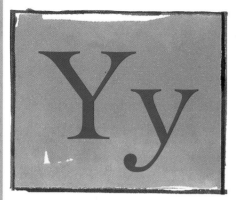

Yy

Y is for yaourt (YOW-out).

Yaourt is the French word for "yogurt." Yogurt and other dairy products are very popular ingredients in French desserts. Yogurt is made by adding friendly bacteria to milk. The bacteria change the milk into a thick, smooth, creamy treat.

FAST FACT: CHEESE, ANOTHER MILK PRODUCT, IS SERVED AS A DESSERT IN FRENCH RESTAURANTS.

Z is for Zoe (ZOH-ee).

Zoe is a popular French name for girls. Other favorite girls' names are Sophie, Helene, and Chantal. Yves, Jean-Claude, Andre, and Philippe are common names for French boys.

FAST FACT: TWO-PART NAMES, LIKE JEAN-CLAUDE, PAUL-HENRI, ANNE-LAURE, OR MARIE-ÉLISE, ARE COMMON IN FRANCE.

France in Brief

Official name: France

Capital: Paris

Official language: French

Population: 60 million

People: mostly French, with several ethnic minorities, such as Celtic and Latin, Teutonic, Slavic, North African, Indochinese

Religions: about 80 percent Roman Catholic; small groups of Muslims, Protestants, and Jews

Education: All children are required to attend school from age 6 to 16.

Major holidays: New Year's Day (January 1); Easter (March/April); Labor Day (May 1); Ascension (May); Bastille Day (July 14); All Saints' Day (November 1); Armistice Day (November 11); Christmas Day (December 25)

Transportation: trains, cars, airplanes

Climate: People inland experience cool winters and mild summers, while those along the Mediterranean Sea have mild winters and hot summers.

Area: 218,812 square miles (547,030 square kilometers)

Highest point: Mont Blanc, 15,771 feet (4,807 meters)

Lowest point: Rhône River delta, 6.6 feet (2 meters) below sea level

Type of government: republic

Most powerful government official: president

Major industries: machinery, technology, chemicals, cars, aircraft, textiles, food processing, tourism

Natural resources: coal, iron ore, zinc, uranium, timber, fish

Major agricultural products: wheat, cereals, sugar beets, potatoes, grapes, beef, dairy products, fish

Chief exports: machinery, aircraft, plastics, chemicals, pharmaceutical products, iron, steel, beverages

National symbol: Gallic rooster

Money: euro

Say It in FRENCH

good-bye . . . . *au revoir* (oh rev-WAH)

please. . . . . *s'il vous plait* (SEE VOO PLAY)

thank you . . . . *merci* (mair-SEE)

one . . . . *un* (UH)

two . . . . *deux* (DUH)

three . . . . *trois* (TWAH)

yes. . . . . *oui* (WEE)

no . . . . *non* (NOH)

Glossary

Allied forces–countries united against Germany during World War II, including
France, the United States, Canada, Great Britain, and others

architecture–a style of building

D-Day–June 6, 1944, the day Allied forces began their invasion of France to free the
country from the Germans during World War II

fluently–clearly and smoothly

fraternity–a group of people with the same interests

habitat–a place with the food, water, shelter, and space an animal needs to live

monarchy–a kind of government in which one person, such as a king or queen, rules

prehistoric–long ago, before stories were written down

resources–things people sell or use, such as wood and oil

To Learn More

At the Library

Costain, Meredith. *Welcome to France*. New York: Chelsea House Publications, 2001.

Fontes, Justine. *A to Z France*. Danbury, Conn.: Children's Press, 2004.

Knoell, Donna L. *France*. Minneapolis: Capstone Press, 2002.

Landau, Elaine. *France: A True Book*. Danbury, Conn.: Children's Press, 2000.

On the Web

FactHound offers a safe, fun way to find Internet sites related to this book. All of the sites on FactHound have been researched by our staff.

1. Visit *www.facthound.com*
2. Type in this special code for age-appropriate sites: 1404815686
3. Click on the FETCH IT button.

Your trusty FactHound will fetch the best sites for you!

Index

LOOK FOR ALL OF THE BOOKS IN THE COUNTRY ABCS SERIES: